Full STEAM Ahead!

Science Starters

Choose to Reuse!

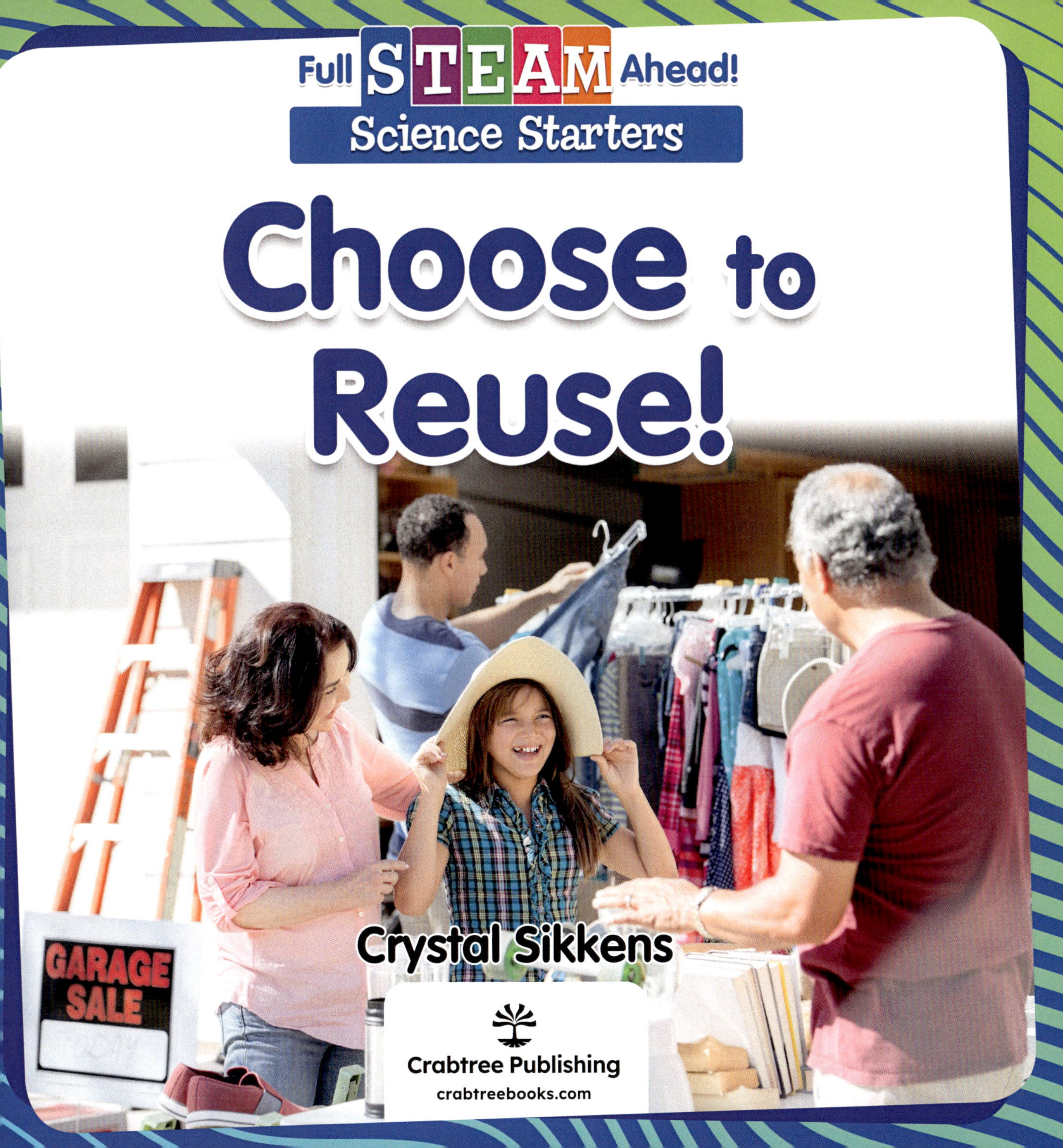

Crystal Sikkens

Crabtree Publishing

crabtreebooks.com

Title-Specific Learning Objectives:

Readers will:

- Understand that people create harmful waste.
- Describe how we can reduce waste using the 3Rs: reduce, reuse, recycle.
- Identify the reasons the author gives to explain how waste affects the environment, and how we can help.

High-frequency words (grade one)	Academic vocabulary
by, can, did, from, how, make, they, with	landfill, plastic, recycle, reduce, reuse, soil

Before, During, and After Reading Prompts:

Activate Prior Knowledge and Make Predictions:

Write these sentences on the board:

- A plastic water bottle can last 1,000 years.
- Most people create 4 pounds (1.8 kg) of trash every day.
- Plastic bottles can be made into clothing.

Ask children to vote on whether they think each statement is true or false. (All are true.) Next, have them read the title of the book. Ask them what they think the book will have to do with the activity they just completed.

During Reading:

After reading pages 8 to 12, ask children to describe the term "single-use plastic" in their own words. Ask:

- How is single-use plastic harmful?
- What examples did the author use to help explain that idea?

After Reading:

Ask students to restate the three ways of helping the environment that they learned about in the book. (Reduce, reuse, recycle.) Divide them into groups and have them brainstorm ways they could start using one of these methods right away.

To Palmer Elizabeth Foxton. Lots of love from Aunt Crystal.

Author: Crystal Sikkens

Series Development: Reagan Miller

Editors: Bonnie Dobkin, Janine Deschenes

Proofreader: Melissa Boyce

STEAM Notes for Educators: Bonnie Dobkin

Guided Reading Leveling: Publishing Solutions Group

Cover, Interior Design, and Prepress: Samara Parent

Photo research: Crystal Sikkens and Samara Parent

Production coordinator: Katherine Kantor

Photographs:
Alamy: Barry Diomede: title page
iStock: therpsihora: p. 4 (l); karayuschij: p. 12; mightyisland: p. 13 (t)
Shutterstock: ingehogenbijl: p. 17

All other photographs by Shutterstock

Library and Archives Canada Cataloguing in Publication

Title: Choose to reuse! / Crystal Sikkens.
Names: Sikkens, Crystal, author.
Description: Series statement: Full STEAM ahead! | Includes index.
Identifiers: Canadiana (print) 20190231750 |
Canadiana (ebook) 20190231785 |
ISBN 9780778772392 (softcover) |
ISBN 9780778771784 (hardcover) |
ISBN 9781427124562 (HTML)
Subjects: LCSH: Recycling (Waste, etc.)—Juvenile literature. | LCSH: Waste minimization—Juvenile literature. | LCSH: Environmental protection—Juvenile literature. | LCSH: Sustainable living—Juvenile literature.
Classification: LCC TD794.5 .S55 2020 | DDC j363.72/82—dc23

Library of Congress Cataloging-in-Publication Data

Names: Sikkens, Crystal, author.
Title: Choose to reuse! / Crystal Sikkens.
Description: New York : Crabtree Publishing Company, 2020. |
Series: Full steam ahead! | Includes index.
Identifiers: LCCN 2019053025 (print) |
LCCN 2019053026 (ebook) |
ISBN 9780778771784 (hardcover) |
ISBN 9780778772392 (paperback) |
ISBN 9781427124562 (ebook)
Subjects: LCSH: Waste minimization--Juvenile literature. | Recycling (Waste, etc.)--Juvenile literature.
Classification: LCC TD792 .S55 2020 (print) | LCC TD792 (ebook) |
DDC 363.72/82--dc23
LC record available at https://lccn.loc.gov/2019053025
LC ebook record available at https://lccn.loc.gov/2019053026

Table of Contents

Crabtree Publishing

crabtreebooks.com 800-387-7650

Published in Canada
Crabtree Publishing
616 Welland Avenue
St. Catharines, Ontario
L2M 5V6

Published in the United States
Crabtree Publishing
347 Fifth Avenue
Suite 1402-145
New York, NY 10016

Printed in Canada/012025/CP20250101

Harmful Waste

Sarah is excited about her birthday party. She has balloons and goody bags for her friends. She has **plastic** cups, straws, plates, and forks for food and drinks.

What Sarah doesn't know is that many of these party items become waste. Waste can **harm** the **environment**.

Waste is anything that is thrown away. After Sarah's party is over, she helps her parents clean up. They throw away the used items.

Our Environment

The environment is everything around us. It includes the air, water, and land.

Look around your environment. What other living things do you see there?

Plants, animals, and people all need a clean environment to stay healthy.

Sometimes the things we do or use harm the environment. A sick environment can hurt us too.

Single-Use Plastic

Many of Sarah's party items are made of single-use plastic. This means they are used once and then thrown away.

Single-use plastic items include plastic shopping bags and drink bottles. Can you think of other single-use plastic items?

Most trash is taken to a **landfill**. It is put into a deep hole and covered with soil. This trash sometimes harms the environment around it.

Landfill trash can harm the environment by **polluting** it.

Ocean Trash

Sometimes plastic is left on the ground. It can also be blown from landfills by the wind or washed away by rain. This plastic often makes it way to oceans, lakes, and rivers.

Plastic trash can pollute water and land.

Animals that live in or near water might eat the plastic or get trapped in it. This can hurt or kill them.

Some animals mistake plastic trash for food.

Plastic Problem

Did you know some pieces of plastic can take up to 1,000 years before they disappear completely?

Over time, waste can disappear, or break down, in the environment. Some types of waste, such as pieces of food, break down easily. Plastic is a type of waste that takes a very long time to break down.

So, what can we do to help take care of the environment? We can **reduce**, **reuse**, and **recycle**!

Reduce

To reduce means to use or buy less. When we reduce, we have less waste.

Using cloth bags instead of plastic bags at the store can reduce waste.

Try to pack a school lunch that has no waste. Put food in containers instead of using single-use plastic bags. Carry a reusable lunch box.

Packing a waste-free lunch is one way to reduce waste at school. Another way is to reuse paper instead of throwing it away.

Reuse

When we reuse we also reduce. To reuse means to use something again or in a new way.

Water bottles can be reused as flowerpots. Then you don't have to buy as many pots. Using water bottles in new ways also reduces waste.

Toys or clothes you don't need can be used by someone else. That means less waste.

People buy and sell used items at yard sales.

Recycle

Did you know plastic bottles can be made into T-shirts? They can when they are recycled! Recycling is taking old items and making them into something new.

We recycle by placing items into recycling bins.

Paper, glass, and plastic are just a few things that can be recycled and made into new items.

Newspaper can be recycled and made into many new things.

Using the 3Rs

What could Sarah do to reduce the waste from her party? How could she reuse and recycle?

reusable plates, cups, and forks

goody bags that can be recycled

reusable boards instead of balloons

Reduce, reuse, and recycle are often known as the 3Rs. Help your family and friends find ways to use the 3Rs.

The environment needs everyone's help to stay healthy!

Words to Know

environment [en-VAHY-ruhn-muhnt] noun Surroundings including air, water, land, and buildings

harm [hahrm] noun To hurt

landfill [LAND-fil] noun A hole in the ground where trash is placed and covered with soil

plastic [PLAS-tik] noun A material that is easily shaped and used to create many objects

polluting [puh-LOOT-ing] verb Making dirty, especially with harmful waste

recycle [ri-SAHY k*uh*l] verb To take an old item and make it into something new

reduce [ri-DOOS] verb To buy or use less

reuse [ri-YOOZ] verb To use again or in a new way

A noun is a person, place, or thing.

A verb is an action word that tells you what someone or something does.

An adjective is a word that tells you what something is like.

Index

About the Author

Crystal Sikkens has been writing, editing, and providing photo research for Crabtree Publishing since 2001. She has helped produce hundreds of titles in various subjects. She most recently wrote two books for the popular Be An Engineer series.

STEAM Notes for Educators

Full STEAM Ahead is a literacy series that helps readers build vocabulary, fluency, and comprehension while learning about big ideas in STEAM subjects. *Choose to Reuse* helps readers identify the reasons and examples used by the author to support key ideas about waste and the environment. The STEAM activity below helps readers extend the ideas in the book to build their skills in science and technology.

Reuse It!

Children will be able to:

- Brainstorm ways to repurpose an everyday item and create a new technology.
- Compare solutions with peers.

Materials

- 5 empty egg cartons
- 5 empty plastic pint or liter bottles
- 5 paper towel or toilet paper tubes
- Choose to Reuse Worksheet
- Choose to Reuse Project Directions Worksheet

Guiding Prompts

After reading *Choose to Reuse*, ask children:

- How can trash and waste be harmful?
- What are the 3Rs? Why are they important?

Activity Prompts

Have children look at the photograph on page 16. Point out that because someone thought of a new use for a water bottle, the bottle did not end up as waste!

Tell children that they will now have a chance to reuse an unwanted item. Divide children into groups of three. Give each group an empty egg carton, a plastic bottle, or a paper tube.

Explain to children that they will create a new technology with the item they are given. Review the definition of a technology, and talk about some examples.

- A technology is anything that makes life easier, safer, and more fun.

Give children time to brainstorm ideas and record them on the Choose to Reuse Worksheet. If they need help, here are some possibilities:

- egg carton: paint cups, seed starter, organizer for small objects
- plastic bottle: bird feeder, pet-food scooper, noisemaker
- paper tube: pencil holder, shaker, binoculars

Extensions

- Give children the opportunity to practice writing clear directions. Hand each group a Choose to Reuse Project Directions Worksheet. Tell them to write directions with pictures that will help others create the new technology they came up with.

To view and download the worksheets, visit **www.crabtreebooks.com/resources/printables**